THE BOOK
OF PEBBLES

FROM PREHISTORY TO
THE PET SHOP BOYS

Written by Christopher Stocks

Illustrated by Angie Lewin

Thames & Hudson

First published in the United Kingdom in 2019 by
Random Spectacular, an imprint of St Jude's Gallery

This edition first published in 2020 by Thames & Hudson Ltd,
181A High Holborn, London WC1V 7QX

Text © 2019 Christopher Stocks
Illustration © 2019 Angie Lewin
Design by Luke Bird
Artwork photography by Jamie McAteer

British Library Cataloguing-in-Publication Data
A catalogue record for this book is available from the British Library
ISBN 978-0-500-02375-4

Printed and bound in Slovenia by DZS-Grafik d.o.o.

To find out about all our publications, please visit
www.thamesandhudson.com.
There you can subscribe to our e-newsletter, browse or download
our current catalogue, and buy any titles that are in print.

Frontispiece: *Flints and Feathers*
Watercolour, 2018

CONTENTS

FOREWORD   6

1   ON CHESIL BEACH   16
2   SIR MORTIMER AT WAR   24
3   PICASSO'S PEBBLES   30
4   JIM EDE AND THE LOUVRE   38
    OF THE PEBBLE
5   BASICALLY DEREK   46
6   EMINENT VICTORIANS   52
7   AT THE NATURAL HISTORY   62
    MUSEUM
8   NO STONE UNTURNED   70
9   SOME PEBBLES   76
10 SOME BEACHES   86

AFTERWORD   102

ACKNOWLEDGEMENTS   108

BIBLIOGRAPHY   110

INDEX   112

SALTHOUSE

on the scenic

NORTH NORFOLK COAST

FOREWORD

SHORELINE, SEA AND SKY

ANGIE LEWIN

A smooth striped stone found in the bottom of my coat pocket transports me back to a beach walk. I can hear the pebbles crunching underfoot, and imagine the view out to sea as I make my way slowly along, scanning the tideline, which is tumbled with shells, driftwood, seaweeds and tattered feathers. A purple-black twist of dried bladderwrack alongside a striated silver and blue-grey pebble is a trigger for a sketch in which I try to capture the coastal landscape.

Each walk seems to have a different focus. One day I'll seek out hagstones; another striped or hooped pebbles. The next day the beach may have a hoard of spherical white quartz pebbles, chalky sea glass or smoothly rounded pottery shards. Pottering on

Salthouse poster
Linocut, 2010

a beach or delving into the life of rock pools could be thought of as a childish activity, but I find it completely absorbing. Time can stand still, a feeling that's heightened if you're lucky enough to have a beach to yourself. Whole days spent outdoors walking and sketching are the best of times for me.

For many years pebbles have formed a backdrop to the native plants that I depict in my linocuts, screen prints, wood engravings and watercolours. Their weathered, ageless solidity creates a visual counterpoint in my pictures to layers of windswept grasses, skeletal plant forms and translucent feathers. Increasingly pebbles have moved into the foreground in my prints and paintings. In linocuts and wood engravings I stylise them, accentuating their graphic qualities and creating pattern by repeating their subtle variations of texture and form.

In 1998 we moved out of London to the north Norfolk coast, and each day I'd walk along the beach. Pebbles shift and move with the tides, and often I'd wake to find the beach transformed overnight by a storm, with steep banks of shingle built up or smoothed flat, or perhaps a series of semicircles scooped out along the length of the beach by the strength of the sea. The striped and speckled pebbles of Salthouse and Cley and the flint and chalk pebbles at Weybourne soon came to define this landscape for me. These long, exposed beaches of shingle fading into the distance create a bleakly beautiful landscape, framed by the grey North Sea.

Alexanders
Wood engraving, 2003

Persephone Shore

Mixed media collage, 2013

Now that we live in Scotland, the beaches of the north-eastern and north-western coasts appear frequently in my work. I love the view from the dunes behind Findhorn Beach, with its banks of striped and ringed pebbles in subtle shades of greys, and across the waters of the Moray Firth to the distant mountains of Sutherland. Gannets plummet into the sea and eider ducks bob on the waves. On North Uist in the Outer Hebrides, the gneiss pebbles are up to three billion years old, making them some of the oldest rocks on earth. Scattered across the white sand, the pebbles have strongly contrasting stripes and range from pale grey to blue-black; in summer the brightly coloured flowers of the machair grow among them. Wild carrot, thrift, yellow rattle, kidney vetch and magenta orchids sing out against the monochrome pebbles. These plants are tough despite their fragile appearance, and I love trying to capture their softness against the stone and the dramatic sea and sky.

Perhaps I can trace collecting natural objects for my home and studio back to the day in the early 1980s when, wandering through Cambridge with a school friend, we tried ringing the doorbell at Kettle's Yard, having no idea of what lay inside. Jim Ede's placing of two flints close to a painting by Alfred Wallis, or a seed pod and pebbles on a shelf alongside a Ben Nicholson were a revelation to me, illustrating how art relates to the natural world and how both are integral to our domestic daily life. I could imagine the tactile experience of choosing the near-spherical grey pebbles on the shoreline, then assembling them on a simple wooden table to create a perfect spiral in gradations of size and shade.

My pebbles are scattered on windowsills and studio shelves alongside my collection of chipped cups and bowls, and they're just as beautiful and valued. I'm no geologist, but I'm attracted by how they look and feel in the hand, and that inspires me to sketch them. In the same way that I've slowly learned more about our native wildflowers by drawing them, I've slowly learned more about pebbles too. My interest is sparked by their relationship with the flora around them and the views to rocks, sea and sky beyond. Along with the tiniest, most insignificant plant, a pebble defines an entire landscape for me, and through them, I try to depict the wild places that I love.

Angie Lewin, Edinburgh

Right: *The 1937 Coronation Mug*   Overleaf: *Autumn Spey*
Linocut, 2005   Lithograph, 2008

ON CHESIL
BEACH

Listen! you hear the grating roar
Of pebbles which the waves draw back, and fling
Matthew Arnold, *Dover Beach*, 1867

Sometimes at night I lie in bed and listen to pebbles being made. The sound is uncanny, yet oddly comforting, like the slow, deep breath of a slumbering giant – or more prosaically, as they used to say on the Isle of Portland, like everyone in Weymouth swishing their curtains open and closed at the same time; but that was in the days of brass curtain-rings. For many years I lived on the Isle, in an old Portland-stone house looking out over Chesil Beach, the vast, semi-detached sweep of pebbles that is one of the wonders

Moonlit Shore
Wood engraving, 2018

of the Dorset coast. Chesil Beach is a strange and compelling place, detached from the land for much of its eighteen-mile length and heaped with pebbles, at its Portland end, to a height of nearly fifty feet. But strangest of all is the mystery – still not satisfactorily explained – of how its stones are graded from east to west.

For the pebbles of Chesil Beach are remarkable not so much for their composition (most of them are flint or chert, harder than steel) as for the way the waves and the tides have graded them consistently in size. It's often been said that, even at night, local fishermen could tell exactly where they had come ashore along the beach's length simply by stooping down and feeling how big the stones were at their feet. Eighteen miles to the west of Portland, where Chesil Beach is generally taken to start, the pebbles are the size of peas, soft and yielding underfoot. At its eastern, Portland end, immediately below my house, they're bigger than a fist, mostly flattened ovals in shape, and extremely uncomfortable under bare feet, which is one reason it stays uncrowded here even on an August bank holiday. I swim from the beach as often as I can, though simply walking down to the sea's edge can be a challenge in itself, for the beach is steep and the large, round pebbles roll against each other, pitching you left and right as you walk, grating together and squeaking like chalk scraped across a blackboard.

We're accustomed to thinking of the sea as a constantly changing thing, but anyone who lives by a beach knows how its shape can shift from month to month and week to week. When the wind blows in a certain direction, or the swell is particularly long, the sea spends its time obsessively refashioning the beach, sometimes altering its contours overnight. On Chesil, high tides and strong winds leave their traces as a series of storm ridges – parallel bands of pebbles, some high, some low, receding for mile after mile until they're lost in the distant salty haze. Just occasionally, when the wind blows from the west and the tides are right, deep scallops form along the water's edge, each of them identical in shape and size. Within each scallop the sea swirls round, over and over, rolling a few more pebbles smooth. Their repeated forms, as your eye takes in the great concave curve of the beach, resemble the notched teeth of a saw.

In its bulk, its size and its extent, Chesil Beach may look eternal, but in geological terms it's of astonishingly recent date, having formed, it's thought, only around 10,000 years ago. Not only that, but the beach we see one year is substantially different to the beach we see the next, and sometimes – as after a big storm – substantially different to the beach we saw the day before. Heraclitus was right: everything that seems to be fixed and eternal is actually in a process of constant change. The blue of the sky may be the same blue I saw yesterday, last year and when I was a child, but every day that same blue is produced by different atoms, different waves of light, different amounts of water molecules in the air. And so it is with Chesil Beach. The chances of seeing the same pebbles by the shoreline from one day to the next are infinitesimally small.

When people ask me why I wanted to write a book about pebbles, my answer has always been the same: how could I live by Chesil Beach and *not* want to write a book about pebbles? Like the leaves on the trees they're ubiquitous yet rare. There are billions of pebbles on Chesil Beach, yet every one is different from every other – different in shape or marked in a different way. But unlike leaves, pebbles have weight and heft, their smooth shapes seeming almost designed to be held in the hand. They're cool to the touch yet comforting to hold. They're free but precious, too: a favourite pebble can become a talisman, a minor household god, a Beckettian worry bead, even a smug little social signifier. They can be as refined as the most delicate Brancusi sculpture, yet they're also as tough as nails. This sculptural quality is, I believe, the key to much of their popularity today. Reduced enough in scale to sit comfortably on the shelves of the smallest flat, their smooth curves and subdued colouration give them a striking resemblance to miniaturised Barbara Hepworths or Henry Moores – which is perhaps hardly surprising, for as we'll see, pebbles inspired some of their finest sculptures in the first place.

The pebbles of Chesil Beach may not be as beautiful and varied as some, but the first thing casual visitors seem to do when they come here is what they do when they visit any shingle beach: pick a handful of them up. If they're male, the next thing they do is to chuck them, one by one, into the sea, where – if the day is calm – they make a satisfying 'plop'. Other, more thoughtful types plod slowly along, staring intently at their feet, in search of the perfect pebble to carry home, though on Chesil this is frowned upon, since the beach is said to be in gradual decline, its source of raw materials cut off long ago by the headlands to the west. Yet people have been taking pebbles from Chesil for thousands of years, as Sir Mortimer Wheeler discovered almost a century ago.

Above: *Longshore*
Linocut, 2003

Overleaf: *The Beach, Aldeburgh*
Linocut, 2005

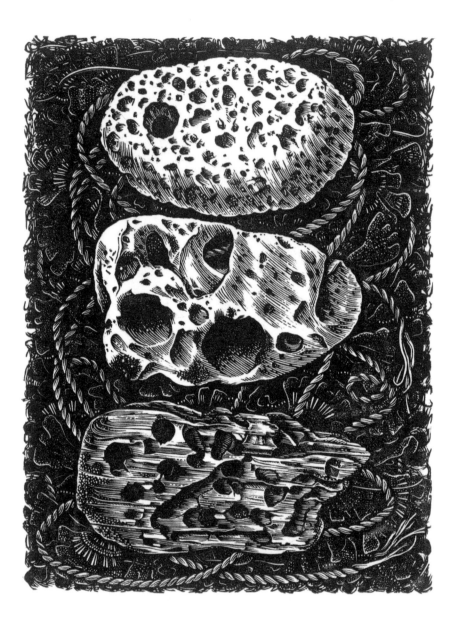

2

SIR MORTIMER
AT WAR

Perhaps our deepest and simplest connection to pebbles is the urge to throw stones. For those with a strong arm and a good aim, pebbles can make lethal weapons, and their offensive use has been recorded in cultures around the world, from David and Goliath onwards. Portland itself was called 'the Isle of Slingers' by Thomas Hardy, referring to the islanders' supposed prowess at slinging stones in self-defence, though this seems to be an undocumented (if relatively plausible) fantasy on Hardy's part. Yet during the 1930s, just a few miles inland, tens of thousands of pebbles were discovered heaped together near the eastern gate of Maiden Castle, the giant Iron Age hill fort near Dorchester, during Sir Mortimer Wheeler's excavations of the site.

Beachcomber
Wood engraving, 1995

Wheeler believed that the pebbles – which ranged from around half an ounce to two ounces in weight – had been carried up from Chesil Beach to be used as sling shots in a doomed attempt to defend the fort against Roman attack. It was a story that captured the public imagination so successfully that, despite Wheeler's conclusions having been cast into doubt by subsequent research, his narrative lingers on in the popular imagination. In an early example of public participation, visitors were actively encouraged to watch the archaeologists at work, and some of the costs of the dig were offset by the sale of postcards, site reports and, it seems, even the pebbles, which reportedly sold for a penny each. One entertaining but sadly unsubstantiated allegation has it that Wheeler replenished the pile occasionally with fresh supplies from Chesil Beach.

Wheeler's assumption that the Maiden Castle pebbles had been gathered with martial intent is an interesting one. He may well have been right, but as a more recent commentator has noted, he doesn't seem to have considered other, more peaceful (if less exciting) uses to which the pebbles could have been put. It's possible, for example, that they had been gathered with a much more mundane use in mind, such as repaving the entrance way, like the heaps of gravel that play such a hallowed role in the iconography of roadside lay-bys today. But in the mid-1930s the thunderclouds of war were gathering, and the idea of conflict was, perhaps, more likely to spring to mind as a way of explaining the pebble pits (especially for a man who, like Wheeler, had fought in the First World War) than it might to archaeologists today.

This page: *Sea Pinks, Island Shore*
Lithograph, 2015

Overleaf: *Saltmarsh Storm II*
Screenprint, 2017

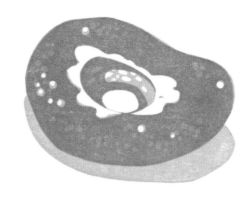

Three pebbles
Linocut, 2018

3

PICASSO'S
PEBBLES

Though Sir Mortimer gave pebbles a romantic allure that also happened to be in tune with his times, from his point of view they were still just raw materials, not so much interesting in themselves as for the uses to which they were put. Yet I think that most of us today look at pebbles rather differently, as beautiful objects in their own right. It's a way of seeing that most of us take for granted, but like most ways of looking at things it has a story of its own, whose origins can be traced back, by one of those happy quirks of history, to a similar time as Wheeler's excavations at Maiden Castle. This new way of seeing was pioneered not by an archaeologist, but (like so many other new ways of seeing, before and since) by artists, and it can be traced back to two particular years, and even to two particular beaches. The years were 1928 and 1930, and the beaches were in Brittany and Norfolk.

The idea that it is through artists we learn to see the world in new ways has become something of a cliché, but in the case of pebbles it seems perfectly plausible. In late July 1928, Pablo Picasso began incorporating pebble forms into a series of beautiful pen-and-ink drawings he made at Dinard, the holiday resort in Brittany where he had taken his wife for a summer holiday (largely, it has to be said, so he could clandestinely meet his teenage mistress, Marie-Thérèse Walter). Picasso later explained his theory of how pebbles and found objects might have inspired the earliest art. 'It seems strange to me that someone thought of making marble statues,' he told his friend and fellow pebble enthusiast, the Hungarian photographer Brassaï. 'I understand how you could see something in the root of a tree, a crack in the wall, in an eroded stone or pebble. But... how could Michelangelo have seen his *David* in a block of marble? Man began to make images only because he discovered them nearly formed around him, already within reach.'

While Picasso was enjoying the *plage* at Dinard, on the other side of the English Channel, the young Henry Moore was collecting flints. Several members of Moore's family had moved to Norfolk from Yorkshire during the 1920s, and its fast-eroding shingle and pebble beaches, with their long lines of low cliffs, were to feed quite literally into his work. In 1930 he suggested to his friend Barbara Hepworth that she and her then husband, the artist John Skeaping, take a summer holiday in Happisburgh (pronounced Hazeborough), a small village on the North Sea coast. The couple rented Church Farm, overlooking the village pond, and they invited Moore and his wife Irina to stay, as well as the painter Ivon Hitchens. Like Henry Moore, Barbara Hepworth was apparently

already attuned to the artistic potential of pebbles. Though her earlier sculptures were largely figurative rather than abstract, in the April 1930 issue of the *Architectural Association Journal*, she suggested that, 'If a pebble or an egg can be enjoyed for the sake of its shape only, it is one step towards a true appreciation of sculpture'.

Moore, for his part, had been pondering pebbles for years. In a 1937 article for *The Listener* called 'The Sculptor Speaks', he recalled that, 'Although it is the human figure which interests me most deeply, I have always paid great attention to the natural, such as bones, shells and pebbles... For several years running I

Hagstones
Pencil drawing, 2003

have been to the same part of the sea-shore – but each year a new shape of pebble has caught my eye, which the year before, though it was there in hundreds, I never saw. Out of the millions of pebbles passed in walking along the shore, I choose to see with excitement only those that fit in with my existing form-interest at the time. A different thing happens if I sit down and examine a handful one by one. I may then extend my form-experience more, by giving my mind time to become conditioned to a new shape… Pebbles show nature's way of working stone. Some of the pebbles I pick up have holes right through them.'

The holiday was a great creative success, not least because of the alluring ironstone pebbles that Moore, Skeaping and Hepworth found on the otherwise mainly sandy beach. Though rarely more than an inch thick and a foot in length, these pebbles proved perfect for carving: fine-grained, neither too hard nor too soft, and easy to polish to a gentle shine. All three sculptors exhibited ironstone sculptures on their return to London, and Hepworth recorded collecting four large crates full of pebbles from Happisburgh to use for future work. The following September, Hepworth and the Moores returned to the village again, minus Hepworth's husband but plus Ben Nicholson (minus his wife). It was to prove a fateful encounter: Hepworth and Nicholson quickly fell in love, and within months they had left their respective spouses and were living together in London. By this point pebbles were so much on Hepworth's mind that, in a letter to Nicholson shortly after he left Happisburgh, she even compared his head to 'the most lovely pebble ever seen'.

The Beach, Salthouse (detail)
Linocut, 2008

Hepworth's first fully abstract sculpture dates from shortly after this second holiday, and before long both Moore and Hepworth began using holes as compositional elements in their work, almost certainly suggested by those hole-pierced flints and pebbles that Moore found so intriguing. But what I find most interesting in his commentary is the sentence, 'Out of the millions of pebbles passed in walking along the shore, I *choose* to see with excitement only those that fit in with *my* existing form-interest at the time.' It reads almost as if Moore was consciously trying to reprogram his eyes, to force himself to look in a new and different way – which I guess is exactly what an artist (or a poet, or a writer) has to do in order to develop a fresh way of seeing the world.

Pebbles remained an important point of reference for the rest of Henry Moore's life, as visitors to his house at Perry Green in Hertfordshire will have seen: pebbles are scattered everywhere you look. For a while they were taken up by other artists too. Whether it was something in the air, or simply the ever-increasing speed of dissemination through magazines and newspapers, but pebble forms insinuated themselves into a number of other artists' work around the same time, from Salvador Dalí's *Accommodations of Desire* of 1929 and Paul Nash's photographs of Dorset pebbles in the early 1930s to the more abstracted organic shapes of Jean Arp. You could say they were the ideal Surrealist object: fluid in shape yet hard, mysterious and mute. Yet for all that, their wider artistic influence was relatively small and short-lived. Picasso, as always, absorbed their lessons and quickly moved on, but Henry Moore stayed faithful to them to the end – and it was through Moore that pebbles-as-art would reach what, for many people, is their apotheosis, though in Cambridge rather than Perry Green.

Windswept Shore
Lithograph, 2015

4

JIM EDE AND THE LOUVRE OF THE PEBBLE

Moore's friendship with art curator Jim Ede started in the 1930s, when Ede and his wife Helen lived at 1 Elm Row in Hampstead, which, as Ede later recalled, was 'a very beautiful Georgian house to which a varied and large circle of people liked to come', including Ben and Winifred Nicholson, Barbara Hepworth and Henry Moore, who lived further down the hill in Parkhill Road. Ede trained as a painter at the Slade, but then worked for the National Gallery and, from 1920 to 1936, as assistant curator at the Tate Gallery, where he championed contemporary artists such as Brancusi and Picasso, often against bone-headed institutional resistance. He became friends with many artists and over the years amassed a considerable collection of paintings and sculpture.

Pebble Spiral
Wood engraving, 2018

But art wasn't Ede's only interest. Writing in the 1940s, he recollected how he 'had always been arranging rooms, either my own or other people's, and once talked over the air [i.e. on the radio] on how to furnish a room. My thought was that the one thing a human being really needed was a room to live in, and scarcely any human being lived in one, it lived on him. I advocated clearing it of everything, and furnishing it with the light and air which were its nature; wonderful empty rooms all over Britain, havens of rest in an over-complicated life.' At this distance it's hard to assess just how important his influence was on British interior decoration, but I think it's fair to say that he was an early exponent of the clear, minimalist, Scandinavian style that would not really come into general circulation until forty years later.

Jim Ede took early retirement at the age of 41 because of bad health, and in 1935 he and Helen left Britain and moved to Tangiers, on the edge of which they bought some land and built a small modernist house called White Stone. During the Second World War they divided their time between Morocco and the United States, where Jim gave successful lecture tours on art and culture. They left Morocco in 1952 and for the next four years they lived in France, but in 1956 they moved back to England to be closer to

Calendula, Teabowl and Flint
Watercolour, 2018

their daughters. They settled in Cambridge, where Jim had been to school, and bought four derelict cottages, which they turned into a single house with the help of a local architect; they named it Kettle's Yard after a sign in the passageway. The Edes lived there for the next fifteen years, during which time Jim continued to build up his art collection, opening the house to students on weekday afternoons. In 1966, after several unsuccessful attempts, they gave the house and their collections to Cambridge University, and in 1973 they retired to Edinburgh, where Helen died four years later; Jim Ede died in 1990 at the age of 94.

In his radio talk on furnishing a room in 1931, Jim claimed that, 'On the whole I find myself preferring to have [no pictures and ornaments], or at most one or two, placed in such a way that I can enjoy them. A picture standing on the floor generally looks better than hanging on the wall…' He also suggested that it was better to 'Have an empty mantelshelf' than one with twenty objects on it, unless each of those objects is there for a special purpose'. But by the time the house started opening to the public, it was overflowing with not just paintings and sculpture but also furniture, glass, pottery – and pebbles. Sebastiano Barassi, the former curator of collections at Kettle's Yard, describes how, 'During the London years, Ede had also developed an interest in found and natural objects, which was deeply rooted in the artistic milieu of Hampstead (Barbara Hepworth and Henry Moore in particular). Ede was a keen collector of all sorts of natural objects, and his friends often gave him shells and pebbles, sometimes sending them from remote parts of the world. Many of these became part of the permanent display at Kettle's Yard, as Ede believed that their presence would enhance the beauty of the works of art by juxtaposition and comparison. The role of natural objects in the house is in fact so crucial that the poet Ian Hamilton Finlay once called it the "Louvre of the pebble".'

Visitors to Kettle's Yard today are often taken as much by Ede's carefully arranged pebbles as they are by the works of art themselves, even though those arrangements have inevitably changed subtly over the years. Talking of the beautiful spiral fashioned from almost spherical grey pebbles, carefully graded for size, which is one of the first things you encounter on entering the house, former assistant curator Mike Tooby recalls that 'We would constantly remake that. And then the precise nuance of the relationship between that and that and that, whatever it might be, might be just slightly different.'

Though Kettle's Yard remains a relatively modest visitor attraction in terms of numbers, its influence on the way we think about pebbles has spread far further thanks to books and magazines, and these days one can hardly leaf through an interiors story about the home of an artist or any other creative type without noticing collections of pebbles artfully arranged on a shelf. As Jim Ede once said, 'It is salutary that in a world rocked by greed, misunderstanding and fear, with the imminence of collapse into unbelievable horrors, it is still possible and justifiable to find important the exact placing of two pebbles.'

Overleaf: *Mug with Yellow Rattle and Yarrow*
Watercolour, 2012

5

BASICALLY
DEREK

There is one final player in what we might call the aesthetic apotheosis of pebbles that we haven't considered yet, and that's the artist and film-maker Derek Jarman, whose wooden shack in Dungeness became a semi-sacred site for pebble-lovers everywhere. Jarman and Jim Ede could hardly have been more different, yet it turns out that there was a direct connection between the two men. In 1971 Jarman was commissioned to design the sets for Ken Russell's film *Savage Messiah*, based on Ede's biography of the artist Henri Gaudier-Brzeska, and as part of his research he visited Kettle's Yard. Perhaps surprisingly, the visit appears not to have been a great success, as Jarman found the intimacy of the place unsettling, perhaps because it was still Jim Ede's home at the time; it can't have helped that Jarman

Seedheads and Hagstones
Watercolour, 2018

apparently found Ede's portrayal of Gaudier-Brzeska a little too hagiographic for his taste. But still I wonder whether the aesthetic of Kettle's Yard got under Jarman's skin, for his own collections of natural objects, though rather more gothic than Ede's, have a remarkably similar feel.

Dungeness attracted Jarman for its weird, desolate beauty. Dominated by the vast, malevolent bulk of a nuclear power station, it is one of the largest and most complex shingle spits in Europe, and its makeshift huts and houses, most of them erected without planning permission and many converted from old railway carriages, evidently appealed to Jarman's self-identification as a sexual and cultural outsider. In the early 1980s the huts also had the advantage of being cheap: when Jarman bought Prospect Cottage with a small inheritance in 1986 it cost £750, including a few extra yards of shingle around it. He spent much of the last eight years of his life living and working in this four-room shack, and gradually transformed the area around it into a rough and ready garden, growing the few plants that could survive the harsh salt winds and lack of water, framing and surrounding them with large flint pebbles (which Jarman called dragon's teeth) and driftwood salvaged from the beach. At Dungeness, unlike Chesil, it's fairly easy to find pebbles pierced with holes, and Jarman threaded these on string to make garlands, which he hung inside the house and on poles around the garden. The pebbles had talismanic properties for him: 'The stones,' he wrote, 'especially the circles, remind me of dolmens, standing stones. They have the same mysterious power to attract.'

Beach with Alexanders

Wood engraving, 2005

Jarman's growing reputation as a counter-cultural icon turned Dungeness into a place of pilgrimage, and in 1995, the year after Jarman's untimely death, Thames & Hudson published *Derek Jarman's Garden*, beautifully photographed by Howard Sooley, which introduced Jarman's pebble assemblages to a far wider and more receptive audience than any he'd enjoyed during his lifetime. You could say that 1995 was the year that pebbles as art objects finally went mainstream – or as Jarman's friend, the Pet Shop Boys singer Neil Tennant, joked a few years later, 'We have Derek to blame for pebbles, really. If you go to a hotel and there are pebbles in a fucking jar, it's basically Derek.'

Polwick II (detail)
Linocut, 2012

6

EMINENT
VICTORIANS

Yet if most people can appreciate the sculptural beauty of pebbles today, that's not to say it's the only way of looking at them. It also begs the question of how people looked at pebbles in the past – in pebbles' pre-history, if you like. We know that Sir Mortimer Wheeler regarded them primarily as archaeological evidence (not to mention a useful source of extra petty cash), but why, in *David Copperfield*, does the infant David help the doomed Little Em'ly pick up pebbles on Yarmouth beach, and what do they see in them? Dickens, unhelpfully, doesn't explain, but it was evidently something children did then just as much as they do today. And in William Dyce's high-Victorian painting, *Pegwell Bay, Kent – a Recollection of October 5th 1858* (now in Tate Britain), are the two well-dressed women adding pebbles to their little wicker baskets, or only fossils and shells?

Christopher's Pebbles
Watercolour, 2018

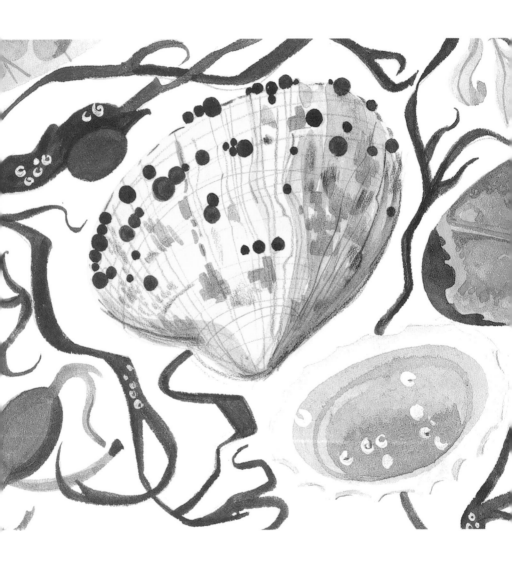

Rockpool Finds
Watercolour, 2011

We can only guess, but there's also a more sober and serious way of regarding pebbles, and that's to look at them, not from the perspective of an artist, but as they're seen by a geologist. It may be the less popular paradigm today, but it has a much longer history, and before Pablo Picasso and Henry Moore started reprogramming their (and our) eyes, I suspect that most educated people looked at pebbles, if they looked at them at all, as geological specimens.

The science of geology was, by and large, a Scottish invention of the late eighteenth and early nineteenth century, and before the advent of deep drilling, the best places to learn about rocks in the raw were quarries, mountains, mines – and beaches. It was, famously, the coastal cliffs at Siccar Point in Berwickshire that convinced John Hutton, the father of modern geology, that his theory of 'uniformitarian' geological development was correct. Coastal erosion reveals geological history in all its glory, and generations of geologists, professional and amateur, have honed their craft on British beaches, hammers in hand.

Early geologists put a lot of effort into classifying fossils, rocks and minerals and making geological maps, but it wasn't until 1859 that pebbles got their first literary evangelist, in the person of the Devon-based naturalist, John G. Francis. His *Beach Rambles in Search of Seaside Pebbles and Crystals*, published by Routledge, Warne & Routledge as part of their Popular Natural History series, was aimed squarely at the educated amateur, and reflects the enormous popularity of collecting and categorising natural specimens, whether animal, vegetable or, in this case, mineral. In setting out his stall, Francis points out that 'while the marine shells of England have been all numbered and classified, and even the seaweeds are emerging out of dim confusion into the order of botanical arrangement, there is no popular work extant on the subject of our pebbles.' It's a charming little book, complete with a section of full-colour illustrations by W. S. Coleman showing polished pebbles, sliced in half to reveal their complex inner worlds, and it must have encouraged many readers to look more closely on their visits to the British coast. †

Beach Rambles offers a rare and fascinating insight into the Victorians' attitude towards pebbles. For a long time the nineteenth century was dismissed as a purgatory of smoke and stovepipe hats, blacking factories and bewhiskered patriarchs in funereal suits, but as visitors to their surviving houses and lovers of their art know, the Victorians also harboured an almost childish delight in bright colours, filigree ornament and highly polished surfaces. This evidently applied to pebbles too. Today we may treasure the pale Modernist palette of pebbles as we find them on the beach, but what John Francis and his contemporaries wanted to reveal was the often brilliant colours of the stone beneath. For this you need your pebbles cut and polished, though, and a thriving cottage industry of lapidarists grew up to service the demand from amateur collectors. Francis describes one of these lapidarist's shops, once common in coastal towns, which sold not just polished pebbles but also gemstones and fossils, its interior dominated by 'a massive semicircular dresser of elm or maple, some four feet in height, and perhaps half as many in width. This is heaped with specimens culled from various beaches, and several convenient shelves are similarly adorned; the polished stones lying in open trays, but set at an angle so as best to reflect the light.'

Behind the shop was a workroom, where the cutting and polishing was actually done. Francis explains the delicate and arduous process, involving numerous wheels and applications of diamond dust, and even suggests how much it would cost to set yourself up in business. Reading his book, the appeal of cutting and polishing becomes easier to understand, as he describes his 'great pleasure in seeing fine pebbles of my own polished. You can stop the wheel every now and then, and watch how the stone gets on. When the chiaroscuro begins to come out on the coloured pattern, the effect is like that produced by holding some lively object before a mirror. The surface no longer appears flat; but you obtain aerial perspective, as in a good painting.'

† Beach Rambles *isn't strictly the first British work of pebbleology. That distinction goes to* Thoughts on a Pebble, Or, a First Lesson in Geology, *by Dr Gideon Algernon Mantell, MRCS, LLD, FRS. Mantell was an obstetrician as well as a distinguished amateur geologist and dinosaur hunter, who among other things was responsible for naming the Iguanodon. But his book, first published in 1836, limits itself to the singular pebble of its title, and for all its charms, is almost entirely concerned with fossils rather than pebbles.*

Overleaf: *Driftwood*
Wood engraving, 1995

7

AT THE NATURAL
HISTORY MUSEUM

Beach Rambles is a reminder that the same thing can often be looked at in several different ways, and that these approaches can change over time, with old ways of seeing (to use John Berger's phrase) being gradually supplanted by new ones – though the old ways sometimes continue to coexist with the new. Pebbles can be sculptures, or paintings, or weapons, or geological specimens, though in their raw state it turns out that they're of less immediate use to a geologist than they might, to an untutored eye, appear. When we first started researching this book, Angie Lewin and I booked an appointment to see the Natural History Museum's then curator of mineralogy, Peter Tandy. Enthusiastically bearded, with his clothes in an apparently chronic state of mild

disarray, Tandy embodies the Platonic ideal of a geologist, and his office, which appeared to have been inexpertly hacked out of the leftover spaces behind and between the geological galleries, was reassuringly overburdened with heaps of boxes and books.

I'd brought along a few favourite pebbles of my own, in the hope that he might seize on them with squeaks of scientific delight, but it turned out in that, at least, I was to be disappointed. Sitting at his desk, I spread them out between us, waiting expectantly for his response. None there came: he cast a professional eye over my prize specimens, then explained that pebbles are difficult to identify in their natural state – precisely the form in which I most enjoy looking at them. Though it's often easy to see which class of rock they belong to, the greyish crust that forms during their long exposure to the salty waters of the sea more often than not obscures their internal structure. The answer, of course, is to don a pair of protective goggles, grab a geological hammer and crack the pebble open, but as that was the last thing I wanted to do to my favourite keepsakes, it became apparent that we had reached a bit of an impasse.

Not wanting to abandon our interview so easily, I asked whether he was often called on to identify things by members of the public like me. Oh yes, he replied, people were always bringing in odd bits of rock. Apparently the commonest delusion among the rock-wielding public is that they have stumbled across a meteorite, though sadly these are vanishingly rare. Not long ago, Tandy told us, he'd received a call from the front desk downstairs, to let him

Aldeburgh Pot
Lithograph, 2013

know that a gentleman had come in with what he thought was probably a meteorite fragment. It was half term, and Tandy had to battle his way through thick clots of schoolchildren to get to the main entrance, where his visitor was waiting for him with a misshapen lump of heavy, metallic rock.

Tandy could tell straight away that it was unlikely to be a meteorite, though he couldn't work out what it was, so he asked if he could take it away for analysis. Of course, the man said. He explained that he'd found it on the Lido in Venice, and what intrigued him was that you could hear something rattling about inside if you shook it vigorously enough, which he proceeded to do next to Tandy's ear. Thinking it most likely – given where it was found – to have been part of a boat that had dropped off and lain on the seabed for many years, Tandy thanked his visitor and took the lump back to his desk. His initial probings and proddings proved inconclusive, so he called up a colleague in metallurgy to ask if they could do a scan. By all means, came the reply, so off the lump went. A day or two later, not having heard anything back from the department of metallurgy, he phoned to ask if they'd worked out what it was. Ah yes, they said. It's in a bucket of water in the yard right now while we wait for the bomb squad to arrive. Far from being a meteorite, it turned out to be a badly corroded Italian hand-grenade, probably from the Second World War. Never let it be said that the life of a mineralogist is dull.

Seaweed Shore
Wood engraving, 2016

8

NO STONE
UNTURNED

Hand-grenades aside, perhaps it's about time to take a look at how pebbles are made and what they're made of – though first it would help to define what a pebble actually is. That sounds simple enough in theory, but like an irritatingly large number of apparently obvious questions, the answer turns out to be 'it depends who you ask'. For there is no universally accepted definition of what constitutes a pebble rather than, say, a boulder or a rock. *The Oxford English Dictionary* defines a pebble as 'A small stone (less than a boulder or cobble) worn and rounded by the action of water.' That seems clear enough, but try going into a little more detail and the picture starts to blur. In the Krumbein phi scale, first published by the American geographer William C. Krumbein in 1937, pebbles are defined as ranging from four to

Stormy Beach (detail)
Screenprint, 2014

sixty-four millimetres in diameter. On the alternative ISO 14688-1:2002 granular scale, however, pebbles don't even get a mention, though cobbles, boulders, gravel, sand and silt all do. But let's not get too hung up on size: we may not be able to explain exactly why, but the fact is that we can all recognise a pebble on the shore, and the *OED* definition is good enough for me.

The pebbles that we pick up on the beach, briefly arresting their journey through the great grinding-mill of nature, may seem inert and dead: simple inorganic matter, without the spark of life that animates all living things. Yet like people, pebbles have different lifespans, governed in pebbles' case not by genes, diet and social circumstance but by factors like hardness and location, and their lives are full of incident – at least until we interrupt the process by taking them home. The longevity of a soft chalk or mudstone pebble on an exposed beach may be measured in weeks, while a chert pebble high on a Mediterranean strand may 'live' for tens of centuries or more. But just as we can safely say that none of us is getting any younger, there is one thing that unites all pebbles, whatever their makeup or situation, and that is that none of them are getting any bigger.

Halfway between being boulders and sand, pebbles start their lives as rough lumps of rock, eroded by glaciers, by rivers, frost or waves, that are slowly washed down to the sea. Turning and turning, tumbled and rolled against each other by river currents or the tide, their sharp edges are gradually worn down, their rough surfaces smoothed off. This incessant action, over tens, hundreds or thousands of years, reduces even the hardest pebbles eventually to dust, or at least to sand. If all pebbles were made of smooth, consistent material they would naturally wear down to near-perfect spheres like marbles. But pick up a few pebbles on the beach and it quickly becomes apparent that the vast majority of them are oval rather than round, and this reflects the internal structure of different kinds of rock. Thus fine white chalk will quickly become smooth and spherical, but just as quickly wear away to nothing; a hard limestone, built up from flat layers of strata, will be worn more slowly, and remain elliptical for far longer. Many of the most sculptural pebbles I've found are flint, whose knobbly, misshapen forms tend to become, if anything, more pronounced and baroque as they get worn down by the sea – the miniature Henry Moores that Henry Moore collected for his own inspiration. I have flint pebbles that look like knucklebones or femurs, primitive earth-mother fetishes and even a polar bear.

Each kind of rock, in other words, will have its own trajectory as a pebble, and to a lesser extent its own character and own colour – though as Peter Tandy explained, that tends to be masked by a greyish glaze of salt. The irony, as we have seen, is that the quickest way of identifying your pebble is to destroy it, but it's still possible to make some educated guesses with the help of the naked eye, a splash of water and a magnifying glass.

Overleaf: *Wooden Dish with Uist Pebbles*
Watercolour, 2016

9

SOME
PEBBLES

This book is mainly about the beauty of pebbles, not their geology (for that see Clarence Ellis's thorough-going *The Pebbles on the Beach*, republished in 2018 by Faber and Faber), but some basic knowledge surely adds to the pleasure of pebble collecting. Here, then, are a few of the commonest types of rock you're likely to find as pebbles on the shore, taken from examples in our own collections.

QUARTZ

This beautiful white, almost translucent pebble looks like an oval moon, and is a type of quartz, formed from tiny hexagonal crystals of silica. In my eyes, the hairline fractures in its surface only add to its beauty. Quartz can be as clear as glass – when it's known as

Tideline Feathers
Wood engraving, 2018

rock crystal – but it more commonly comes in a range of colours, from white and pale yellow to pink and brown. Though pebbles of pure quartz are attractive in themselves, as a mineral it is also found in almost every kind of rock, most strikingly as those often parallel white stripes in slate and limestone. Quartz is hard: so hard, in fact, that while most pebbles can be scratched with a knife, a piece of quartz will scratch glass.

BRICK, GLASS AND CONCRETE

If there's one thing that draws us to the seashore more than anything else, surely it's the fact that here, on a small island, you can be pretty sure of finding nature in the raw. We think of beaches as wild and untrammelled places, but human activity has a way of infiltrating even the most natural-looking spots in unexpected ways. Coal turns up on beaches in County Durham, for example, swept there from the mines at Easington, while soft-edged sea glass can be found wherever bottles have washed up on shore or gone down with a ship. Small lumps of concrete break off tank traps and other wartime structures that were often built cheaply and quickly on the beach, using local materials wherever possible. Brick is another man-made material that you'll occasionally find on the beach, where it's quickly worn down to smooth, ovoid or rather flat pebbles that feel pleasantly soft and chalky to the touch. Though they're most often found near towns, so many brick structures have toppled over cliffs that they can turn up almost anywhere, though generally in fairly small quantities.

Shoreline Finds
Watercolour, 2018

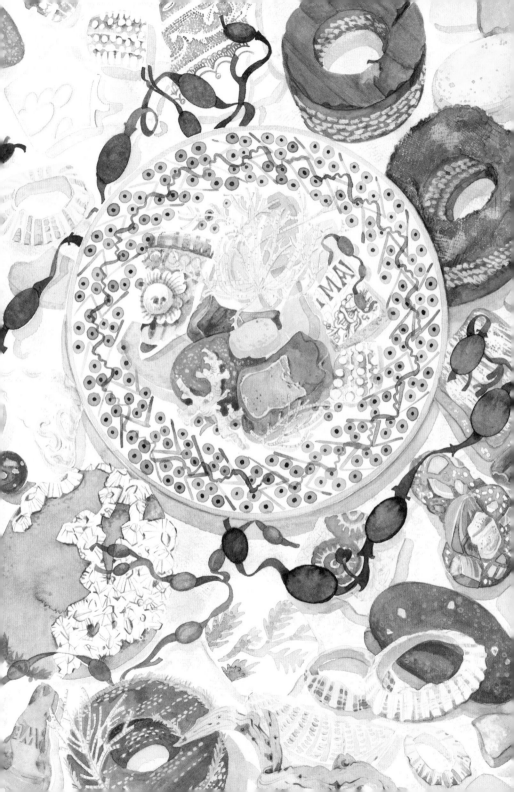

LIMESTONE

Dove grey, smooth and etched with a beautifully subtle pattern of parallel lines, this is one of my favourite pebbles, and it's made from limestone. Limestone comes in many forms and shades, but its generally grey or whitish colour is only emphasised by the salt glaze that coats pebbles on a beach. It's a widespread rock in the British Isles, and has always been one of our most important building stones. I may be biased, but Portland is perhaps the finest limestone of all: chalky white, fine-grained and easy to carve, it has been used for so many buildings in London, from St Paul's Cathedral to the whole of Regent Street, that it's said there's more Portland stone in London now than is left on the Isle of Portland itself. Different types of limestone vary in hardness, from chalk – which wears down so quickly that chalk pebbles rarely last long on a beach – to extremely hard crystalline forms.

SANDSTONE

The soft oxblood pink of this pebble reveals it to be made of sandstone, probably from South Devon, where it's widely used as a building stone. In its 'natural' form, without a pebble's grey salt glaze, this New Red Sandstone (as it's called to distinguish it from the Old Red Sandstones of North Devon) is a fierce pinkish-red, and the city of Exeter, which was once largely built of it, must have seemed astonishingly ruddy to first-time visitors. Sandstone, of course, is a sedimentary rock, composed from minute rounded grains of sand that themselves were ground down from other rocks many millions of years ago. Though many sandstones are quite pale in colour, the most striking varieties are red. Their colour derives from the inclusion of feldspar or iron oxide, better known on metal as rust. As Jacquetta Hawkes wrote in her classic account of British geology, *A Land*, 'Much of the New Red Sandstone still glowing warmly through Midland rain was laid down in great lakes or land-locked seas that covered central and northern England at a time when the surrounding lands were sun-baked deserts.' You can almost feel the warmth in the rock.

FLINT

Flint is a fascinating and rather mysterious material, as we're still not entirely sure how it forms. It's found as nodules within sedimentary rocks, which then erode from the cliffs containing them – a process that can be seen quite dramatically in the chalk cliffs at Beachy Head and the Needles on the Isle of Wight, where bands of glossy black flints protrude from the dazzling whiteness of the chalk. Flints are made from an extremely hard kind of quartz, which is thought somehow to fill small gaps between larger masses of other rocks, and their striking, knobbly shapes (which can make them look like sun-bleached bones) probably follow the contours of the void in which they formed. Though they often have a brilliantly white or yellowish outer coating, their quartz interiors are dark grey and glassy in appearance. Because they're so hard, flint pebbles can end up dominating a beach after pebbles of softer rocks have worn away. They're also among the best sources of hag stones – pebbles with holes through them, which were once nailed to cottage doors to ward off witches and other undesirable passers-by.

GRANITE

This rough, angular pebble, speckled pink and grey, is a type of granite that formed far underground, cooling slowly enough for crystals to form. These crystals are a feature of many granites: generally speaking, the larger the crystals, the longer the rock took to cool and the more time crystals had to grow. Their origins, deep within the earth, mean that crystalline granites are usually hidden beneath other rocks, and are only revealed after millions of years of erosion have worn the overlying rocks away. In Britain, the largest areas of granite are found in Scotland and Cornwall, whose quarries have supplied kerbstones to city streets since the coming of the railways, and it's on their beaches that granite pebbles are most likely to be found. Their hardness, and their granular texture, mean that they're rarely smooth or smoothly rounded.

SLATE

Pebbles are rocks in disguise, their original colours and shapes softened and blurred by time and tide. But most rocks resist this process to some degree or other, which is why so many are oval rather than perfectly round, and some resist it in particularly distinctive ways. Few rocks on the beach are as obvious as slate, which splits into thin layers, and tends to produce strikingly flat grey pebbles, however rounded their outlines might become. This makes them perfect skimming stones, which explains why the World Stone Skimming Championships take place in a flooded former slate quarry on the Scottish island of Easedale every year.

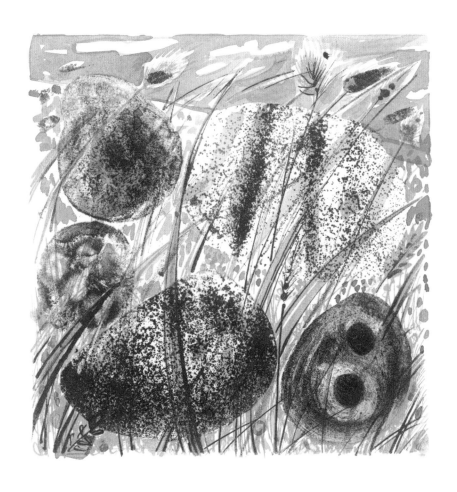

Windswept Shore
Early proof with watercolour, 2015

SCHIST

Like slate, schist is a metamorphic rock, created when sedimentary shales and mudstones are subjected to intense pressure and heat. Like slate, too, it can easily be split along fracture lines to make roof slates and floor tiles. But while slate retains the fine-grained grey appearance of the sedimentary silt from which it was originally formed, in schist, further heating and pressure produces flat grains of minerals such as mica and quartz, which catch the light and give schist its distinctive shimmering quality. This silvery sheen helps identify schist pebbles, along with their often strongly defined layers, which can look almost like the grain in wood.

GNEISS

At first glance pebbles of gneiss (pronounced 'nice') could be taken for granite, but they are easy to distinguish because, unlike granite, they have stripes. Yet though layers generally suggest sedimentary rocks such as limestone and sandstone, gneiss (like schist) is actually metamorphic, and is formed when other rocks – which could be sedimentary, volcanic or metamorphic in origin – are recrystallised under conditions of enormous pressure and heat. These crystals separate into bands, giving gneiss its distinctive appearance. Because it is extremely hard, gneiss pebbles are usually oval or roughly spherical.

Gneiss Pebbles, Berneray
Watercolour, 2018

10

SOME
BEACHES

Mainland Britain has something like eleven thousand miles of coastline, which is longer relative to its size than almost any other nation in the world; Spain, more than twice Britain's size, has less than half its length of coast. Britain's geology is as complex as its shape, and its beaches form a spectacular showcase for the hundreds of different rock types found around its shores. Here are a few of our personal favourites.

ST COLUMBA'S BAY
IONA

Though it can only be reached by foot or by boat, St Columba's Bay is well worth the effort, not least because it is one of the most

Harris
Linocut, 2007

colourful beaches in the country. On the southern tip of Iona in the Inner Hebrides, this sheltered cove is covered with pebbles of pink, red, orange, grey and green, which include coral-coloured granite and striped Lewisian gneiss, which has the distinction of being the oldest rock in Britain, dating back some 2.7 billion years. You can also find white Iona 'marble' (actually a kind of limestone) and, most famously, so-called 'St Columba's Tears' – small teardrop-shaped nephrite pebbles in vivid translucent green. It's here that, according to legend, St Columba landed in the year 563 after being exiled from Ireland, going on to found the monastery that, for several hundred years, was to be a major centre of Celtic Christianity. Above the western side of the beach are around fifty pebble cairns whose origins are lost in the mists of time, though one theory is that they were built by medieval pilgrims, or by monks atoning for their sins.

WHERRY TOWN
CORNWALL

The Lizard peninsula is the most southerly point in mainland Britain, and one of the best places to find pebbles of serpentine, the green rock that makes up most of the famous peninsula. Many of the beaches here are good pebble-hunting grounds, but perhaps the widest mix of rock types can be found around Penzance. The pebble beach at Wherry Town, between Penzance and Newlyn, abounds in everything from serpentine to quartz-veined slate, jasper, agate, granite, flint, citrine and carnelian, and has the added advantage of easy accessibility for less athletic pebble-hunters.

SHINGLE STREET
SUFFOLK

The clue is in the name. This isolated little scatter of houses on the south Suffolk coast overlooks a steep shingle beach which is also a Site of Special Scientific Interest, with a thriving population of wild sea kale, horned poppies and tree mallows growing beyond the reach of the waves. The beach – mainly composed of flint pebbles – can be thought of as an extension to Orford Ness, the great bank of shingle that blocks the route of the River Alde at Aldeburgh and diverts it ten miles south until it finally escapes into the sea just north of Shingle Street. Accessible only by a single-track road, overlooked by Martello towers and haunted by avocets and little owls, it's a place of beautiful desolation.

CHESIL BEACH
DORSET

One of the grandest and most striking sweeps of pebbles in the country, Chesil Beach dominates an 18-mile stretch of the Dorset coast. This enormous sweep of pebbles begins as a conventional enough beach, but in the eight-mile stretch between Abbotsbury and Portland Harbour it is separated from the mainland by the long, brackish Fleet lagoon. Chesil Beach is a striking example of a tombolo or barrier beach – a spit of land formed by tidal action that connects an island to a larger body of land – and is estimated to contain around 180 billion pebbles, graded by the action of the tides from pea gravel at its western end to large cobbles where it meets the Isle of Portland. It has an unusual

history too. In geological terms it's remarkably recent, probably having been formed only around 10,000 years ago, created by rising sea levels at the end of the last Ice Age. Despite its vast extent, however, it is composed of surprisingly few different types of pebble: predominantly flint and chert, with a scatter of pink and red quartzite pebbles from Budleigh Salterton in Devon, plus smaller pieces of jasper. At first glance it may seem odd that there are few bright orange sandstone pebbles from the cliffs of West Bay or limestone pebbles from the Isle of Portland, even though they stand at either end of Chesil Beach, but the sandstone is too soft to survive the action of the waves for long, and tides sweep most of Portland's stone away from the beach to the east.

Dice Cup and Feather
Watercolour, 2014

RYE HARBOUR
EAST SUSSEX

Though not so striking or as well known as the huge promontory of Dungeness just a few miles further east, the beach at Rye Harbour is attractive not just for its setting, fronting an important nature reserve for overwintering birds, but also for its pebbles, which are varied and colourful, though (like most of the south and east coasts of England) dominated by flints. Among these, if you're lucky, you'll stumble across occasional groups of blue-coloured flint pebbles that appear to have been intentionally gathered together. They're rare survivals of a once-thriving local industry, which supplied ceramics companies as far away as Stoke-on-Trent, where burnt, ground-up flint powder was added as a strengthening agent to clay from the 1720s on; later it was also sometimes used as an ingredient in the manufacture of glass. Blue flints were collected from the beach here as late as the 1930s, in specially adapted 'boulder boats' which transferred their cargo to trains on the Rye Harbour line.

FINDHORN
MORAYSHIRE

The Findhorn River and Findhorn Bay has been a source of inspiration for Angie Lewin for many years, drawn here by the clarity of the light and the wonderful array of striped, circled and speckled pebbles in blues and ochres and greys that are scattered across the beach along with driftwood, feathers and seaweed. Pebbles are found along the river too, where they've scoured potholes out of the bizarrely curved and contorted rock. Beyond the beach a path snakes along the edge of the dunes, where marram grass is dotted with harebells and heather on the landward side, with the mountains of Sutherland rising in the far distance.

PORTMUCK
COUNTY ANTRIM

Like Chesil Beach, the beach at Portmuck is a fine example of a tombolo – a spit of land created by wave action that connects the mainland to an island, though in this case only at low tide. Muck Island, at its far end, is a bird sanctuary, so perhaps it's a good thing that fast-moving tides and slippery rocks make the crossing hazardous. Facing north-east across the Irish Sea, with fine views along the cliff-fringed Antrim coast, it's one of the most attractive beaches in Northern Ireland, with a sandy foreshore backed by large white pebbles, framed by National Trust land on either side.

BLACKFRIARS
LONDON

Central London might be the last place you'd expect to find a pebble beach, but the fast tides that scour the River Thames are perfectly capable of wearing rocks down, though at a slower rate than the constant action of the open sea. At low tide numerous beaches or banks are revealed, and their composition reflects the largely man-made environment around them. Between Blackfriars Bridge and Tate Modern is a particularly good example. Its underlying layer may be mud and London clay, but the surface is scattered with fragments of brick rubble, much of which was dumped in the Thames after the Blitz; in places the brick has worn down to form smooth, soft-red pebbles that (after a good rinse) are very pleasing to the touch. Perhaps more striking are the unexpectedly large white lumps of chalk that can be seen on both sides of the Thames. They puzzled me for years. Could they somehow have been swept downstream all the way from the Goring Gap, where the river cuts through the Berkshire Downs? The answer was finally provided by the excellent Thames Discovery Programme, which explores what the organisation describes as 'the capital's longest archaeological site'. It turns out that chalk blocks were laid on these banks intentionally in the nineteenth century, to form a (relatively) soft base on which Thames barges could rest safely at low tide.

NEWGALE
PEMBROKESHIRE

Newgale is just one of the many beautiful beaches that make the Pembrokeshire coast such a magnet for visitors, but this two-mile stretch of sand just south of Saint David's is unusual in being backed by a huge raised storm beach composed of pebbles, which – the story goes – dates back to the great storm of 25 October 1859. The pebbles are satisfyingly varied in colour and origin, reflecting the area's rich and complex geology, and include examples of volcanic rocks such as yellow rhyolitic agglomerates and smooth porphyritic lava, which date back around 450 million years. This beach separates the sandy foreshore (which is only exposed at low tide) from the A487 trunk road, sheltering it from south-westerly winds, but bigger storms batter the beach and have pushed its pebbles across the road, blocking it for days. With increasingly ferocious storms likely to become more frequent in the future, it's possible that the beach will be pushed further inland and that the road will have to be rerouted, so visit while access is still easy.

SALTHOUSE AND BLAKENEY POINT
NORFOLK

This unique stretch of the north Norfolk coastline may already be familiar to admirers of Angie Lewin's work, since the bleak, exposed landscape with its line of beach, sea and sky was the subject of her earliest prints when she first moved to the county, and she still returns to the beach each year to draw. Blakeney Point forms the end of an exposed shingle ridge, over seven miles long, which begins at Weybourne and is backed by saltmarsh and mudflats. Like so many of the beaches along the east coast of England, it's composed mainly of flint eroded from the underlying chalk, though it also has a scatter of pebbles formed from Norwich red crag, a shelly sandstone found a few miles further east at Sheringham. Around Salthouse the artificial shingle bank that was once constantly repaired by little bulldozers has now been abandoned to the action of the waves, allowing the sea to break through during big storms – after one storm a few years ago a seal was seen swimming along the main coast road.

THURSTASTON
LANCASHIRE

This popular sand and shingle beach on the west side of the Wirral peninsula is backed by low cliffs of yellow boulder clay, which covers much of the Lancashire coast. The pebbles that have eroded from the soft clay of the cliffs have a fascinating range of origins, since they were dragged here by a vast glacier from as far away as south-west Scotland and Cumbria. The glacier carried boulders too, but intriguingly the biggest boulders on the beach seem not to have come from the cliffs; one theory is that they were abandoned here by sailing ships that had used them as ballast.

SCARBOROUGH
NORTH YORKSHIRE

Justly famous, Scarborough's sandy beaches also offer a happy hunting ground for pebble enthusiasts, as they include a rich mix of shingle made up not only of the millstone grit, limestone and shale of the Yorkshire cliffs, but also from rocks that have been swept south along the coast from County Durham, Northumberland and as far north as Scotland. Cornelian Bay, a couple of miles south of the town, is even named after the carnelian pebbles that can sometimes be found there, along with agate and quartz.

Working drawing for Northern Shore (detail)
Mixed media, 2013

TYNINGHAME
EAST LOTHIAN

The coast south of Edinburgh has some wonderful bays, including Tyninghame, approached through pine, oak and rhododendron woods that, in places, overhang the beach. Gnarled roots grip the sand, with pebbles and pine cones mixed together, and the vibrant orange berries of sea buckthorn catching the sun. The beach has a rich variety of different pebbles in reds and greys, some as full of holes as worm-eaten wood, and beyond it rises the rocky headland of St Baldred's Cradle, fringed by weirdly wave- and wind-sculpted rocks.

Though this book explores the allure of pebbles, and most readers will have taken a handful back from the beach, it may come as a surprise to discover that under the Coast Protection Act of 1949 it can be a crime to take pebbles from beaches in England and Wales. Of course it may seem ridiculous that somewhere like Chesil Beach, with its estimated 180 billion pebbles, could be seriously affected by visitors taking a few pebbles each, but the Act was passed with a serious purpose in mind, to reduce the risks of potentially damaging coastal erosion.

Luckily for amateur pebble collectors, it appears that the Act only comes into force if a county or local authority makes an order (which must be confirmed by a minister of state) that applies the Act to a particular beach or section of coastline. Often there will be notices to that effect on the beach in question, but not always, so it is always sensible to try and discover whether a particular beach is protected, and please respect any local signs.

Overleaf: *The Church, Salthouse*
Linocut, 2008

11

AFTERWORD

'I do not know what I may seem to the world, but as to myself, I seem to have been only like a boy playing on the seashore and diverting myself in now and then finding a smoother pebble or a prettier shell than ordinary, whilst the great ocean of truth lay undiscovered all before me.'
Attributed to Sir Isaac Newton

———

I'm lying on Chesil Beach. It's one of those hot late-summer days without a breath of wind, and the sea has a surface like mercury. Yet close to the shore you can see there's still a gentle swell. It's only an inch or two high, but that is enough to drop tons of water on the edge of the beach every five seconds or so. The front of each shallow wave thuds so heavily onto the shore that you can feel the boom of it below you through the pebbles, and as it

Dandelion III
Wood engraving, 2004

withdraws down the steep slope of the beach it drags pebbles with it, which make a weird screeching hiss as they resist. This is my favourite time to swim. The water is glassily transparent, and if you swim out you can see the sea bed quite clearly twenty or thirty feet down, or you can float close to the shore and let the swell pull you gently in and out again. The feeling is like flying: weightless, suspended, unearthly, ecstatic.

Chesil isn't a comfortable beach to lie on, at least at the Portland end: its grey chert pebbles are far too big. They dig into your back and move underfoot, making entry to and exit from the water into an undignified and painful scramble unless you've thought to wear swimming shoes. If I turn my head I can see the great curve of the beach sweeping away towards Abbotsbury Hill and the orange cliffs of West Bay: billions upon billions of pebbles, large here but slowly getting smaller the further west you go. I've been wondering for a long time why we collect pebbles, and I hope this book provides a few plausible ideas, but one final thought occurs to me as I sit here on the shore.

For those of us who don't live on top of a volcano, beaches are probably the most dynamic and changeable environments we know. We may associate them with holidays and pleasure, but they're really sites of entropy and destruction. Right at the start I said that at night I could listen to pebbles being made, but it would be more accurate to say that I hear them being destroyed, as they're slowly ground down to sand by the relentless action of the waves. Could it be that, perhaps without really knowing why, we take pebbles home with us to preserve them, like helping a hedgehog cross a busy road? By taking pebbles away from the beach, we arrest an otherwise ineluctable process of dissolution and decay. It's as if we are trying to stop time in its tracks.

But of course our hopes, if that's what they are, can only prove illusory, for in the long run our actions will make no difference to the onward march of geological time. However far we take our pebbles from the beach (and many of us will have brought a few back from distant holidays), however much we treasure them, we will all, in the end, lose hold of them, and what then? Maybe our successors will return them to the sea, or simply throw them away. A hundred years or more and our houses will fall, and time will slowly move along. As the hundreds turn into thousands and the thousands into hundreds of thousands, earthquakes, glaciers, landslides and volcanic activity will reshape the earth we know, carrying our pebbles with them. Millions of years will pass, and everything we know will be ground down to dust. But that dust, in its turn, will eventually create new rocks. And from those rocks, if rain still falls and the oceans still move to the tug of the moon, new pebbles will form, ready to begin the endless cycle all over again.

Overleaf: *Northern Shore*
Linocut, 2013

ACKNOWLEDGEMENTS

The germ of the idea for this book originally saw the light of day thanks to a great little fanzine with the exquisitely noncommittal title of *Things*, sadly no longer with us, though still available online thanks to the wonders of the internet; my number one thank you, then, must be to Jonathan Bell, who commissioned me to write about pebbles for *Things* before anyone else did. Thank you to Brigitte Carter and Jean-Louis Hurbe for letting me stay in their pebble-filled house in Peillon, where I began to write this book in earnest, and to Steven Horner for introducing me to them; to Angie and Simon Lewin for creating the beautiful illustrations and making the whole publishing process such fun; to Peter Tandy, former curator in the Earth Sciences Department (Mineral and Planetary Sciences Division) at the Natural History Museum, for agreeing to meet Angie and me, who he didn't know from Adam, and for being such an enthusiastic and friendly fount of knowledge on all things mineral, as well as his equally helpful and friendly colleague, Hellen Pethers, in the treasure-filled NHM library; to all the friends who responded to requests for information about local beaches, especially Steven Will; to Helen Randall and her colleagues Ed Rees and Henna Malik for help understanding the legal aspects of pebble collecting; to Deborah Burnstone for giving my manuscript a superbly exacting edit; to my mum, for putting me up and looking after me so well. But first and last to Roy Barker, for putting up with me for all these years.

Seaweed and Seedheads
Wood engraving, 2007

BIBLIOGRAPHY

Barassi, Sebastiano: *The collection as a work of art: Jim Ede and Kettle's Yard* (University Museums in Scotland conference, 2004)

Barber, Janet: *Pebbles as a Hobby* (Pelham Books, 1972)

Chatwin, Bruce: *In Patagonia*, Chapter 95 (Jonathan Cape, 1977)

Ellis, Clarence: *The Pebbles on the Beach* (Faber and Faber, 1954; republished 2018, with a new introduction by Robert Macfarlane)

Francis, J.G.: *Beach Rambles, in Search of Sea-Side Pebbles and Crystals* (Routledge, Warne & Routledge, 1859)

Fullwood, John (1894–1928): *Pebbles Found on British Beaches* (unpublished and undated, in the library of the Natural History Museum)

Hamilton Finlay, Ian: *Unnatural Pebbles, with detached sentences on the pebble* (Graeme Murray Gallery, Edinburgh, 1981)

Hawkes, Jacquetta: *A Land* (Cresset Press, 1951; republished by Collins Nature Library, 2012)

Kay, George: *Collecting Pebbles, Rocks and Fossils* (Beaver Books, London 1980)

Ede, Jim; and others: *Kettle's Yard and its Artists: An Anthology* (Kettle's Yard, University of Cambridge, 1995)

Mantell, Gideon: *Thoughts on a Pebble* (Relfe & Fletcher, 1836)

Munari, Bruno: *The Sea as a Craftsman* (Corraini Edizioni, 1995)

Østergaard, Troels V.: *Rocks and Pebbles of Britain and Northern Europe* (Penguin Books, 1980)

Thornton, Nicholas: *Moore | Hepworth | Nicholson: A Nest of Gentle Artists in the 1930s*, catalogue for exhibition at Norwich Castle Museum and Art Gallery, 2009

Ulrich, Herbert; Schwartz, Walter; and Stuhler, Werner: *Kieselsteine* (Ernst Wasmuth, Tübingen, 1981)

Zalasiewicz, Jan: *The Planet in a Pebble: A Journey into Earth's Deep History* (Oxford, 2010)

INDEX

Abbotsbury, Dorset 89, 104
agate 88, 98
Aldeburgh, Suffolk 89
Architectural Association Journal 33
Arnold, Matthew: *Dover Beach* 17
Arp, Jean 36
Beachy Head, Sussex 81
Beckett, Samuel 20
Berger, John 63
Blackfriars beach, London 93–94
Blakeney Point, Norfolk 95
Brancusi, Constantin 20, 39
Brassaï (Gyula Halász) 32
Brick pebbles 78, 94
Budleigh Salterton, Devon 91
carnelian 88, 96–98
Cornelian Bay, Yorkshire 96–98
chalk 72–73, 94
chert 72, 91
Chesil Beach, Dorset 17–20, 26, 89–91, 103–4
citrine 88
Cley, Norfolk 8
Coast Protection Act 1949 98–99
concrete pebbles 78
Dalí, Salvador 36
Dickens, Charles: *David Copperfield* 53
Dinard, Brittany 32
Dungeness, Kent 48–51

Dyce, William: *Pegwell Bay, Kent* 53
Ede, Jim 11, 39–43, 47
Ellis, Clarence: *The Pebbles on the Beach* 77
Exeter, Devon 80
Findhorn beach, Morayshire 11, 92–93
flint 48, 73, 81–82, 88–89, 91–92, 95
Francis, John G.: *Beach Rambles* 57
Gaudier-Brzeska, Henri 47
glass pebbles 78
gneiss 85, 88
granite 82, 88
hag stones 48, 81
Hamilton Finlay, Ian 43
Hampstead, London 39, 42
hand grenade 68
Happisburgh, Norfolk 32, 35
Hardy, Thomas 25
Hawkes, Jacquetta: *A Land* 81
Hepworth, Barbara 20, 32–36, 39, 42
Hitchens, Ivon 32
holes 35–36, 48, 81, 98
Hutton, John 57
Iona, Inner Hebrides 87–88
Jarman, Derek 47–51
jasper 88
Kettle's Yard, Cambridge 11, 42–43, 47–48
Krumbein phi scale 71
Krumbein, William C. 71
Lewisian gneiss 88
Limestone 73, 80, 88, 96

Listener, The (magazine) 33
Lizard peninsula, Cornwall 88
Mantell, Dr Gideon Algernon:
   Thoughts on a Pebble 59
Maiden Castle, Dorset 25–26, 31
meteorites 68
millstone grit 96
Moore, Henry 20, 32–36, 39, 42, 57, 73
mudstone 72
Nash, Paul 36
Natural History Museum, London 63–68
Needles, The, Isle of Wight 81
nephrite 88
Newgale beach, Pembrokeshire 94–95
Newlyn, Cornwall 88
New Red Sandstone 80–81
Nicholson, Ben 11, 35, 39
North Uist, Outer Hebrides 11
Norwich Red Crag 95
Old Red Sandstone 80
Orford Ness, Suffolk 89
Penzance, Cornwall 88
Perry Green, Hertfordshire 36
Pet Shop Boys 51
Picasso, Pablo 32, 36, 39, 57
Portland, Isle of, Dorset 17–18, 25, 80, 89–91
Portmuck beach, County Antrim 93
Prospect Cottage, Dungeness 48
Regent Street, London 80
quartz 77–78, 81, 98

quartzite 91

Russell, Ken 47

Rye Harbour, Sussex 91–92

Saint Columba's Tears 88

Saint David's, Pembrokeshire 94

Saint Paul's Cathedral, London 80

Salthouse beach, Norfolk 8, 95

sandstone 80–81, 95

Scarborough Beach, Yorkshire 96–98

schist 85

serpentine 88

shale 96

Shingle Street, Suffolk 89

Siccar Point, Berwickshire 57

Skeaping, John 32, 35

slate 82, 88

Sooley, Howard 51

Stoke-on-Trent 92

Tandy, Peter 63–68, 73

Tate Britain 39, 53

Tennant, Neil 51

Thurstaston beach, Lancashire 96

Tyninghame, East Lothian 98

Wallis, Alfred 11

West Bay, Dorset 91, 104

Weybourne, Norfolk 8, 95

Wheeler, Sir Mortimer 25–26, 31, 53

Wherry Town beach, Cornwall 88

World Stone Skimming Championships 82

Yarmouth, Norfolk 53

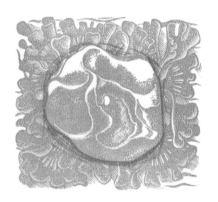

Stone Circle

Wood engraving, 1995